The Husbands

Also by Christopher Logue

WAR MUSIC   *(1987)*

KINGS   *(1991)*

THE
HUSBANDS
An Account of
Books 3 and 4
of Homer's *Iliad*

Christopher Logue

Farrar · Straus · Giroux

New York

Library of Congress Cataloging-in-Publication Data
Logue, Christopher.
The husbands : an account of books 3 and 4 of Homer's Iliad /
Christopher Logue. — 1st ed.
p.   cm.
1. Helen of Troy (Greek mythology)—Poetry.   2. Paris (Legendary
character)—Poetry.   3. Menelaus (Greek mythology)—Poetry.
4. Homer—Adaptations.   I. Homer.   Iliad. Book 3–4.   English.
II. Title.
PR6023.O38H87   1995   821'.914—dc20   95-13117   CIP

ACKNOWLEDGEMENTS

For critical, and financial, support while writing *The Husbands* I am much indebted: for the first, to the late Lindsay Anderson, Liane Aukin, the late Sally Belfrage, Charles Rowan Beye, James Campbell, Jasper Griffin, Ruth Padel, Bernard Pomerance, Craig Raine, and to my editor, Christopher Reid; for the second, to Raymond Danowski and Bernard Stone. As well, I would like to thank Mme Jacques Brel, Hugo Claus, Ian Hamilton Finlay, Alsthair Fowler, Melville Hardiment, Oona Lahr, John Simpson of the Oxford University Press, Christian Smith, Martin Taylor of the Department of Printed Books, Imperial War Museum, and Michael Taylor, all of whom wrote to me or spoke to others on my behalf.

Contents

The Husbands

Prologue

Deceived by God, and abandoned by Achilles, Agamemnon leads the Greeks across the plain for an assault on Troy.

"A drink! A toast! *To those who must die.*"

"On my land, before my sons,
Do you accept this womb, my daughter, Helen, as your wife?"
"I do."
"Her young shall be your own?"
"They shall."
"You will assume her gold?"
"I will."
"Go. You are his. Obey him. And farewell."

Breakfast in Heaven.
Ambrosia alba wreathed with whispering beads.
    *"In the Beginning there was no Beginning,
And in the End, no End,"* sing the Nine to the Lord,
And Hera's eyebrows posit: *"Now?"*
And now Athene goes.

Think of those fields of light that sometimes sheet
Low tide sands, and of the panes of such a tide
When, carrying the sky, they start to flow
Everywhere, and then across themselves:
Likewise the Greek bronze streaming out at speed,
Glinting among the orchards and the groves,

And then across the plain—dust, grass, no grass,
Its long low swells and falls—all warwear pearl,
Blue Heaven above, Mt Ida's snow behind, Troy inbetween.

Troy.
The Acropolis.
The morning light behind the Temple's colonnade.
Then through that colonnade, Hector of Troy,
Towards his mass of plate-faced warriors:
    And your heart leaps up at the sight of him,
And wonders of courage are secretly sworn
As he says:

"Torches and Towers of Troy, the Greeks are lost.
They dare not wait, but are ashamed to go
Home in their ships to their belovéd land
Without our city stowed. Therefore for them:
This desperate advance. Therefore for us:
Trumpets at sunrise from the mountain tops!
Our gods are out! Apollo! Aphrodite! so close,
You taste the air, you taste their breath, a loving breath
That shall inspire such violence in us
Dear hearts, full hearts, strong hearts, courageous hearts,
Relaxing on our spears among their dead,
Heaven fought for us, 100 bulls to Heaven,
Will be our pledge.
    "I put my hands in yours.
Prepare to be in constant touch with death
Until the Lord our God crowns me with victory."
    These were his words,
And knowing what you do you might have said: "Poor fool . . ."
Oh, but a chilly mortal it would be
Whose heart did not beat faster in their breast

As Quibuph set the cloche-faced gull-winged gold
Helmet with vulture feather plumes on Hector's head,
And Hector's trumpeter, T'lesspiax,
Set the long instrument against his lips
And sent:
    "Reach for your oars!"
    "Reach for your oars!"
In silver out across the plain, and then again,
As Hector shook his shoulders out, again, and Hector's throng
Gave a great shout of rage

As down from the Acropolis they flow
And through the streets they press,
While 30,000 Panachean masks
Move on at speed across the plain to Troy.
And what pleasure it was to be there! To be one of that host!
Greek, and as naked as God, naked as bride and groom,
Exulting for battle! lords shouting the beat out
    "One—"
Keen for a kill
    "Two-three"
As our glittering width and our masks that glittered
Came over the last low rise of the plain   and

    "Now"

(As your heart skips a beat)

    "See the Wall."

And you do.

It is immense.

So high

So still

It fills your sight.

And not a soul to be seen, or a sound to be heard,
Except, as on our thousands silence fell,
The splash of Laomedon's sacred springs,
One hot, one cold, whose fountains rise or die
Within a still day's earshot of the Wall,
And inbetween whose ponds the Skean road
Runs down beneath the zigzags of God's oak
Until, under the gate of the same name,
It enters Troy, majestic on its eminence.

Within: Prince Hector's mass,
    Without: a pause, until
Paramount Agamemnon, King of kings,
Lord both of Mainland and of Island Greece,
Autarch of Tiryns and Mycenae, looked,
Now right, now left,
Then at the Wall, then into Heaven, and drew his sword.
And as he drew, Greece drew.
And this disscabbarding was heard in Troy
Much like a shire-sized dust-sheet torn in half.
    A second pause. And then
At Agamemnon's word the Greeks moved on
Down the low hill to Troy
As silently as if they walked on wool.

The gates swing up:
The Skean, the Dardanian, the South.

Hector: "Not yet."

"Not yet."

Then:

"Now."

Think of the noise that fills the air
When autumn takes the Dnepr by the arm
And skein on skein of honking geese fly south
To give the stateless rains a miss:
So Hector's moon-horned, shouting dukes
Burst from the tunnels, down the slope,
And shout, shout, shout, smashed shouted shout
Backwards and forth across the sky;
While pace on pace the Greeks came down the counterslope
With blank, unyielding imperturbability.

25 yards between them.

20.

Then, as a beam before its source,
Hector sprang out and T-d his spear; halted his lines;
Then lowered it; and stood alone before the Greeks

King Agamemnon calls:
"Silent and still for Hector of the soaring war-cry,
The irreplaceable Trojan."

Then hands removed Prince Hector's shield, his spear,
And all Greece saw his massive frame, historical
In his own time, a giant on the sand, who said:

"Greek King: I speak for Ilium.
We have not burned you in your ships.

9

You have not taken Troy. Ten years have passed.
Therefore I say that we declare a truce,
And having sworn before the depths of Heaven to keep our word,
Here, in God's name, between our multitudes,
I will fight any one of you to death.
  And if I die" (this said within an inch of where he will)
"My corpse belongs to Troy and to Andromache;
My body-bronze to him who takes my life; and to you all,
Helen, your property, who was no prisoner,
with her gold.
  And if I live: my victim's plate shall hang
Between the columns of Apollo's porch on our Acropolis,
But you may bear his body to the coast
And crown it with a shaft before you sail
Home in your ships to your belovéd land
With nothing more than what you brought to mine.
  Pick your best man. Commit yourselves to him.
Be sure that I am big enough to kill him
And that I cannot wait to see him die.
Then in their turn crossing our dark-wine sea
Passengers who come after us will remark:
'That shaft was raised for one as brave and strong
As any man who came to fight at Troy,
Saving its Prince, Hector,
Superb on Earth until our Earth grows cold,
Who slaughtered him.' Now who will that Greek be?"

  Answer him, Greece!

  But Greece has lost its voice.

  Thoal is studying the sun-dried heads
And chariot chassis fastened to the Wall.

  Titters from Troy.

10

Then cannon off lord Menelaos': "Me."
"No.   Hector will kill you," from his brother.

Yet he has gone—how could he not!—out
Onto the nearside ground. Alone.

But someone is already there.

Odysseus. The king of Ithaca.

History says,
Before Odysseus spoke he seemed to be,
Well . . . shy—shuffling his feet, eyes down—the usual things.
However, once it passed his teeth, his voice possessed
Two powers: to charm, to change—
Though if it were the change that made the charm
Or charm the change, no one was sure.

The sun gains strength.
Thoal has taken Menelaos' hand.

Odysseus:

"Continuing and comprehensive glory to you both,
Hector, the son of Priam, King of Troy,
Agamemnon, the son of Atreus, my King.
And to us all.

"I dare not speak for Heaven,
But as our Lord, the Shepherd of the Clouds,
Has honoured us by following our war,
Now, through Prince Hector's lips, He seems to say:
    "Let the world flow through Priam's gates again,
And Greece return to Greece with all debts paid."
    Lords of the Earth,

11

We are God's own. Our law is His. Is force.
What better way to end this generous war
Than through the use of force—but force in small:
Not, all to die for one, but one for all.
   The proverb says:
The host requires the guest to make himself at home.
The guest remembers he is not.
This is the reason why no Greek
Dared to pre-empt lord Menelaos' right
To take Prince Hector's challenge, even if—
Greece having sworn to keep the word it gives—
The Lord our God returns him to Oblivion.
   Why wait, then?
   Comrades in arms, here is the why:
Hector has fought and fought, has given blood, and now—
Breathtaking grace—offers his armour and his life to end
The hostilities he did not cause.
   Soldiers! Brave souls! Surely that is enough?
Even lord Schlacht, the hate-hot god of war, says: *True,*
It is enough.
   So who should Menelaos fight . . . ? My friends,
Your silence says: Only fools state the obvious.
And as there's no fool like an old fool, so
It falls to me to state it:

Paris.

The handsome guest . . ."

"Yes."

" . . . the one who started it . . ."

"Yes." "Yes." (and rising)

12

"among us on the plain here . . ."

"Yes!"

". . . who else to face the man whose property he stole,
Soft in his bed up there on the Acropolis?
Paris, with his undoubted stamina,
Will give our Greek a long and vicious fight to death."

"Ave!"

"What fitter culmination to our war,
Or climax apter it to end?"

A beat, and then
The great assembly pleased itself with cheers
That bumped the Wall, and coasted on
Over the foothills and the moony dunes,
The woods and waterfalls of Ida, on—
Bearing their favourite thoughts and plans,
Their *"Peace for me,"* their joy at going home.

"Find him."

No need for that. At Hector's word,
Like dancers on a note, the shields divide,
And there, chatting among themselves, we see
Prince Paris' set; Pandar, his fan; Tecton,
The architect who built his fatal ships—
With Paris in their midst.

Napoleon's Murat had 50 hats
And 50 plumes each 50 inches high

And 50 uniforms and many more
Than 50 pots of facial mayonnaise
Appropriate to a man with tender skin;
He also had 10,000 cavalry,
Split-second timing, and contempt for death.
So Providence—had he been born
Later and lowlier—might well have cast Prince Paris.
   The centuries have not lied:
Observe the clotted blossom of his hair,
Frost white, frost bright—and beautifully cut,
Queen Aphrodité's favourite Ilian.
And though his hands are only archer's hands,
Half Hector's size, his weight half Hector's weight,
He is as tall as Hector (8′9″)
And as he walks towards him, note his eyes
As once his father's were: pure sapphire.

They have not spoken for five years.

"Ah, there you are—"
(Blowing a speck off his brother's plate)
"Sit, sit."

He does.
Aeneas and Chylabborak withdraw.
   "Thank God we did not have you stoned to death
The day you brought her home.
   Will you fight, or not?"

Smoke from the morning sacrifice ascends.
You hear the hymn?

"Hector, your voice is like an axe," his brother said.
"But what you say is true. I brought the Greeks.
But if he kills me, as he may, mind this:

I take no credit for my beauty, or its power.
God gives to please Himself. If He is busy—
Or asleep—one of His family may bless
A mortal soul, in my case Aphrodite.
I have been true to what she gave to me.
Not to have fallen in with Helen
Would have been free, original, and wrong."
   He stands. So debonair!
   "Hail and farewell, dear Ek."

   Then to the lords:

   "See that the armies sit
With spears reversed and armour set aside.
Then put lord Menelaos and myself
Between you, on marked ground, and we shall fight
Until the weaker one, and so the wrong, lies dead.
   Then, having retained or repossessed her, lawfully,
Let her surviving husband lead the beauty of the world,
And what is hers, away.
   As for yourselves: you shall, before we fight,
Baptize your truce with sacrificial blood,
And pray that you may keep the words you give,
No matter who shall live. Then part,
Troy to its precincts and its provinces,
And Panachea in her troop ships home
Across the sea to the belovéd land
Of Greece, of handsome wives."

   Eight o'clock sun. Some movement on the Wall.

   Clouds.

   Clouds.

Unanswerable magnificence.

"Hear me as well," lord Menelaos says.
"One person always comes off worst.
For ten years, me. Never mind that. Though Paris started it,
Everyone here has suffered for my sake.
But now that you have left the war to us
It does not matter which one dies,
Provided, when he has, you part
And ponder on it as you go your ways.
   One other thing. Though I have tried
I cannot bring myself to trust Troy's young.
Therefore, old as he is, and ailing as he is,
I ask for *Priam!* Laomedon's son,
Great King of Troy, the Lord of Ilium,
To come down here onto the plain.
That done, bring lambs—a black for Greece, a white for Troy—
And, watched by us all, old Priam shall
Cut their young throats, and offer Heaven their blood,
For only he is king enough to make
Certain that Ilium keeps what Ilium gives,
And only he, the Lord of Holy Troy,
Adding his voice to ours, can turn those words
Into an oath so absolute
The Lord our God may bless it with His own."

Agreed.

Now dark, now bright, now watch—
As aircrews watch tsunamis send
Ripples across the Iwo Jima Deep,
Or as a schoolgirl makes her velveteen
Go dark, go bright—
The armies as they strip, and lay their bronze

And let their horses cool their hooves
Along the opposing slopes.

Agreed.

But not in Heaven.

Queen Hera: "Well?"
Athene.
   "They are about to swear and sacrifice."
   "So . . ."
Touching the left hand corner of her mouth:
   " . . . they do it frequently," and now the right.
   "A common sacrifice."
Glass down.
   "You mean, together? Greece and Troy? As one?"
   "As one."
Settling her loose-bead bodice. Turning round:
   "Who to?"
   "To Him."
   "What for?"
   "For peace."
   "*Peace*—after the way that Trojan treated us?"
   "Peace, home, friendship, stuff like that."
   "It must be stopped."
   "At once."
   "It will." And so,
With faces like NO ENTRY signs they hurried through the clouds.

Snow on Mt Ida. With Menelaos' wish
Lord Thoal and Chylabborak's son, Kykeon, walk towards Troy.

Troy. Less light. A sweetwood roof.
Sunshine through muslin. Six white feet,
Two sandalled and four bare
    Exit into the passages.

Troy. The atelier. Stitch-frames and large warp-weighted looms
    " . . . Paris is hated . . ."
Right-angled to the sills
    " . . . and so is she."

The passages. Approaching feet. The women hesitate.

"Ah . . . Lady . . ." Soos (Priam's first herald), smiling, says, and bo
Helen, her maids, on by.
    "I see young Nain has fained.
Make sure he joins us on the terraces, Pagif."

An inner court.
Gold loops across the sluiced coclackia.

"All stand."

We do.

    She sits.
She lifts her veil.
She backs her needle out.
    "This is the only time she stops
Thinking of how she looks . . ."

The terraces. Their awnings set since Dawn
Stepped dripping from the sea.
                              And up and in
Between the parapet, the flaps,
Murmuring shimmers drift.

  Soos:
  "Neomab has the plan, Pagif will check the seating,
Nain can watch. King Priam's brothers first. Pagif?"
  "On the back row—"
  "The *highest* row."
  "—the fathers of King Priam's four full-brothers' wives;
Those brothers, and their wives; their brothers, and *their* wives."
  "Excellent."
  "Chrome, King of Macedon; his daughter, Tept,
Their son, lord Akafact, with Hector on the plain . . ."

The atelier. On Helen's frame
  " . . . she will be fought for. In an hour . . ."
Achilles Reaches Troy, a nine-year work
  . . . "To death?" . . .
Whose stitchwork shows that lord
  . . . "With spears." . . .
Tall on the forepeak of a long dark ship,
  . . . "Then they'll make peace." . . .
  "Poo-poo." . . .
Dismantled chariots in its waist.
  He has the kind of look that perfect health,
Astonishing, coordinated strength,
Pluperfect sight, magnificence at speed, a mind
Centred on battle, and a fearless heart display
When found in congruence.
  . . . "What will she wear?" . . .

19

Observe his muscles as they move beneath his skin,
His fine, small-eared, investigative head,
His shoulder's bridge, the deep sweep of his back
Down which (plaited with Irish gold)
His never-cut redcurrant-coloured hair
Hangs in a glossy cable till its tuft
Brushes the combat-belt gripping his rump.
   What does it matter that he brought
Only 1,000 men in 20 ships?
For as they rowed their superchild between
Our 30,000 heavy, upright oars,
"*Achil! Achil! The king,*" they cried,
"*Whose Godsent violence will get us home!*" so loud
The local gods complained to Heaven.

"Lady . . . my lady . . . We must go,"
Cassandra, Priam's youngest girl, says as she lifts
The needle out of Helen's hand, who turns
Towards this serious 13-year-old wife—
As she once was—and lets herself be led
Across dry-by-now coclackia, into stone.
   "There is a huge array . . . thousands of them!
And there's to be a final fight for you.
Not as per usual, though—blood everywhere.
They have calmed down, both theirs and ours,
All sitting quietly—their armour off,
You cannot see the foreslopes for its shine.
And round about the midday sacrifice,
Your two . . . I mean, my brother Paris and—"
   "Yes, yes."
   "Will fight to death for you below the Wall.
But first you must be viewed. You are the property.

20

My father's exarchs want to see the property.
It is their right."

The sweetwood roof.

"Please ask if I can watch."

Cloud, like a baby's shawl.

"How many names, Pagif?"
"200 names."
"And stools?"
"200 stools."
Long rows of them. Silent and void. And suddenly

All full!

Music

An arch of bells,
A tree of china bells,
Two trees of jellyfish and cowslip bells,
All shaken soft, all shaken slow,
Backed by Egyptian clarinets.

And they pass by.

Then quadraphonic ox-horns hit their note,
And as it swims across the plain
Ten Trojan queens
Led by son-bearing Hecuba
Enter
And sit.

A lull.

And then,
And then again, but with a higher note, that note
Instantly answered by a roar of silk
As Asia stands for Laomedon's son
Priam of Troy, the Lord of Ilium
His litter shouldered high, lord Rhesos walking by its couch,
Onto the Skean terracing.

Helen, her maids—Cumin and Tu—wait   off.

Nothing will happen till he nods.

He nods.

Below,
Chylabborak tumbles the lots.

Diomed takes one.
Paris'.
Paris will have first throw.

"We knew it was a fatal day," Tu said,
"Long before Soos announced:
'Now see the beauty to be fought for with long spears'
And Nain said Go, and up we went,
The sweat was running down between my breasts.
But she was braver than Achilles, when,
With only two steps left, she pulled her veil off, yes,
And so did we!—Do not stop there, I prayed,
You carry Aphrodité in your breast,
Pull down your dress and let your body say
Is this not worth a ten-year war?—
But then we reached the top.   And lo!
The sun stood upright in the sky, and from beneath
The murmuring glitter of the plain."

What is that noise?

The fountains?

No, my friend—it is Creation, whistling . . .

Silence and light. Beneath a mile of air
The plain is still.

Then 50,000 faces turn, and tilt,
And sand to sight, the colour of the plain;
And Fate, called love, possessed them.
    Still as it was, the moment grew more still,
As softly, as on holiday, alone,

When seaside zephyrs stir a consecrated grove,
Parting their lips, as one, stressing each syllable
The thousands said:

"Ou nem'me'sis . . ."

"Ou nem'me'sis . . ."

This boy who came from Corinth
Where the water is like wine;
"Ou nem'me'sis . . ."
This man from Abigozor on the Bosphorous;
And this unlucky nobody from Gla.

The terraces.
It is lord Thoal's moment. Soos moves him forward.
Thoal says:

"Favours from God to you, Priam of Asia,
And may the smile He uses to calm storms
Protect our truce.
"When wrong is done, one person always suffers most.
For Greece, lord Menelaos is that one.
He knows that Paris, your good-looking son,
Began, and has continued in this wrong,
But also knows that everyone,
Not least yourself, has suffered for it.
"Therefore, to make as sure as sure can be
That this day is the last day of our war,
Lord Menelaos asks that you, Great Sir,
Come down onto the plain with us,
And sacrifice with us,

25

For you alone are king enough to make
Certain that Ilium keeps what Ilium gives,
And can alone, as Lord of Holy Troy,
Promote those words into an oath, so absolute,
Our Father, God, may bless it with His voice."

The windmills on the Wall are still.
King Priam stands. Then lifts his withered arms, and says:

"To the plain."

And on the plain the drums begin to beat.

White horses on the sea, and on the shore,
Where the passing of the days is the only journey,
    See
The first of the Immortals, known as God,
Strolling along the sand.

Suddenly Lord Poseidon puts his head above the waves:

"Good morning."
"And to you."

A pause. And then:

"Could I have your opinion of the wall?"
"The Wall?"
"The new, Greek, wall."
"You mean their palisade."
"I mean their wall."
"They have begun a palisade, but not a wall.
Walls, as you know, are made of stone," God said

As He resumed His steps.

"And as *you* know," his brother said (wading along)
"We split the world in two.
You got the sky. I got the sea. And the Earth—
Especially what the humans call the shore—
Was common ground. Correct?"

"Correct."

"Then why is Greece allowed to build a wall
Across my favourite bay with nothing said?
Did I hear aves? No. Paeans? Not one.
Pfwah . . . do what you like with Lord Poseidon's honey sand,
No need to sacrifice a shrimp to *him*.
Just up she goes! Renowned as far as light can see!
The god—some seaside lizard sneezing in the weed.
His dignity—a rag. A common rag."

"Brother," God said, "your altars smoke on every empty coast,
To catch your voice grave saints in oilskins lean across the waves.
Try not to let the humans bother you—
My full associate in destiny. Between ourselves"
(Leading him out onto the sand) "I may wind up this war,
And then, Pope of the Oceans, with Greece rowing home
You will have sacrifices up to here . . .
And as they heave, your train of overhanging crests
Obliterates their spade-and-bucket Maginot Line.
But later,—when I give the nod."

Hardly are those words out, when:

"Rubbish!"

They hear, and looking round they see
(Steadying her red-sepal hat with the russet-silk flutes)
Creamy-armed Hera with teenage Athene
(Holding their scallop-edged parasol high)

27

As they wobble their way down the dunes,
Shouting:

    " . . . truce . . ."
    " . . . and an oath . . ."
    "For peace . . ."
    " . . . dirty peace."
    "In your name . . ."

    But as they near their voices fall,
And as they slow their eyes fall, too,
For looking into His when He is cross
Is like running into searchlights turned full on.

    "Imparadise Mt Ida, and," God said,
"Tell Heaven to meet me there,"
Then He was gone. And Lord Poseidon, gone
Backwards into the depths,
His tower of bubbles reaching to the light.

Fierce chrome. Weapon grade chrome
Trembling above the slopes.
And standing in it, leaning on their spears,
The enemies. And overall,
The city's altars, smoking.

    A messenger runs between the lines.

    Then nothing.

    Then a boy selling water.

    Then nothing.

Then nothing.

"Come on! Come *on!*"

Then 50 kings walk through

And greet—

Dressed in a silver-wool pelisse, his crown
Of separate leaves (of separate shades of gold)
Each representing one of Ilium's trees—
As he steps from his car onto the plain,
Priam of Troy. Who says:

"Paramount Agamemnon, from my Temple font,
Accept this pyx of consecrated fire,"
(That Soos holds out)
"Ilium's eternal promise to our Lord,
That Troy shall keep the word it gives,
That when your brother, or my son, lies dead,
Our war will end."

"Ave!"

That is:

"Ave!"

As Thoal and Kykeon slip
Into the line among the younger best
    "Ave!"
A lordly pace, behind these lordly men
As they process between the slopes,
As they process, carrying the black lamb and the white,
King Agamemnon and Prince Hector, both,

29

Behind Dynastic Priam (8'6")
Correctly known as the Great King of Troy
Himself behind a boy, who gives, each second step,
A rim-shot on his drum.

In a plain bowl
Soos and Talthibios mix
Water and wine
Then pour it over Hector's spear-arm hand,
    "Ave!" (but soft—some, trembling)
Then pour
    "Ave!" (so soft—some, weeping)
It over Agamemnon's spear-arm hand.
Then these are dried.
Then Hector takes King Agamemnon's knife
(His feasting knife) and crops a tuft
Of lovely, oily wool from each lamb's nape.
    And when these fingerfuls
(By Akafact for Troy, for Greece Antilochos)
Were taken to the overlords
And each had kept a hair and passed the curl along,
King Agamemnon said:

    "Your terms are granted, Troy.
The woman will be fought for, now, to death.
Paris shall have first throw."

    It is the moment for the prayer.

"My son?"

Prince Hector says:

"God of All Gods, Most Holy and Most High,
Imperial Lord of Earth, Sire of the Night,

And of the Rising Stars of Night, true King
Of waste and wall, and of our faithful selves,
We ask you from our hearts to let us end
Through one just death our memorable war."

This was Prince Hector's prayer,
Tenderly, softly prayed.
And as the silence that came after it
Increased the depth and wonder of the day,
The heroes filled their drinking cups with wine
Sainted with water, which is best, and sipped:
And what in them was noble, grew;
And truthfulness, with many meanings, spread
Over the slopes and through the leafy spears,
As Priam thrust the knife into the white lamb's throat
(Which did not struggle very much) and pressed it down;
And then into the black lamb's throat, and pressed it down;
And then, as the overlords spilt out their cups,
Lifted the pan of blood Talthibios and Zeus had caught,
Bright red in silver to the sun.

"Amen."

And then:

—Two
        —Two
                —Two-three

The drum.

"Amen . . ." (but stronger now) and now
The shin and bodice bronze of those about to fight

31

—"Yes!"—
—"Yes!"—
Is carried up and down the measured ground.

The lords:

"We swear to kill, and then castrate, whoever breaks the oath."

And as the spears, the cymbal shields, the freshly gilded crests,
—"Yes!"—
—"Yes!"—
Are carried round,
The lords:

"*Let both be brave, dear God. Dear God,*
See that the one who caused this war shall die."

Silence again. Then from the blue
A long low roll of thunder, of the kind—
And then again, again—that bears fat drops.
Though no drops came.
Finally, though, the sky stopped muttering. And then,
100,000 palms rose with their voices, and:

"*To you!*"
"*To you!*"

Billowed into the light.

Here comes a hand

That banks

Topples through sunlit music
Into a smoothdownsideways roll

Then

Hovers above Ida imparadised

Salutes the gods, and

Out.

But they just smile. They are the gods.
They have all the time in the world.
And Lord Apollo orchestrates their dance
And Leto smiles to see her son, the son of God,
Playing his lyre among them, stepping high,
Hearing his Nine sing how the gods have everlasting joy,
Feasting together, sleeping together,
Kind, color, calend, kiss, no bar, time out of mind,
And how we humans suffer at their hands
Childish believers, fooled by science and art,
Bound for Oblivion—
Until

TRUMPETS!

SUSTAINED!

Sustained by sunlit chords:

"High King of Heaven, Whose temple is the sky,"

Now the Nine sing, as,
Led by a flock of children through the dance,
God comes, lofty and calm, and lifts His hand.

Then in the hush, but far and clear, all Heaven heard:

"To You!"
"To You!"

"To You!"
"To You!"

The measured ground.

In a fast slouch, the Trojan lord,
With a belligerent snarl, the Greek,
Come on to it.
    Both men stand tall. Both men look large.
And though the Ilians were proud of him,
Paris, his mirror bronze, his hair,
Beautiful as he was, they detested him.
    But heroes are not frightened by appearances.
Under his breath lord Menelaos says:
    "I hate that man. I am going to kill that man.
I want to mark his face. I want to shout into his face:
You are dead. You are no longer in this world."

The drum.

The 50 feet between them. Then:

"Begin."

The Trojan turns.

Five steps.

Re-turns, and right arm back, runs
—Four —three —two
And airs his point for Menelaos' throat.

But heroes are not worried by such sights.
Even as he admired the skill with which
Paris released his spear *"Dear God"* lord Menelaos prayed
"Stand by me" as he watched the bronze head lift
"Think of the oxen I" then level out *"have killed for You"*
And float towards his face. And only then
(As when, modelling a skirt, if childbride Helen asked:
"Yes?" he would cock his head) he cocked his head,
And let the spear cruise by.
        And

—"Yes!"—

Cried the Greeks, and then again
(But by that time their husband's thrown his own)

—"Yes!"—

And he is running under it, as fast as it, and

—"Yes!"—

As the 18-inch head hits fair Paris' shield
And knocks him backwards through the air
(Bent like a gangster in his barber's chair)
Then thrusts on through that round
And pins it, plus his sword arm, to the sand
The Greek is over him, sword high, and screaming:

"Now you believe me! Now you understand me!"

Smashing the edge down *right, left, right,*
On either side of Paris' face, and:

"That's the stuff! That's the stuff! Pretty to watch!"

Queen Hera and Athene shout, as Paris' mask
Goes *left,* goes *right,* and from the mass:

"Off with his cock! Off with his cock!" *right-left,*

And on the Wall: "God kill him," (Helen to herself)
As Menelaos, happy now, raises his sword
To give the finishing stroke, and—cheering, cheering, cheering—
Down it comes: and shatters of Lord Paris' mask.

No problem!

A hundred of us pitch our swords to him . . .
Yet even as they flew, their blades
Changed into wings, their pommels into heads,
Their hilts to feathered chests, and what were swords
Were turned to doves, a swirl of doves,
And waltzing out of it, in oyster silk,
Running her tongue around her strawberry lips
While repositioning a spaghetti shoulder-strap,
The Queen of Love, Our Lady Aphrodite,
Touching the massive Greek aside with one
Pink fingertip, and with her other hand
Lifting Lord Paris up, lacing his fingers with her own,
Then leading him, hidden in wings, away.

Then both slopes looked this way and that and then around,
For there was no one who would hide that man.

And Menelaos is in torment, yes,
Is running naked up and down
Saying things like: "Where did he go?"
"Somebody must have seen him go?" and then
He has gone down on both his knees, naked, on both his knees,
Shaking his fists at Heaven, shouting out:

"God God—Meek, Time-Free Trash,
Your hospitality is mocked.
And so are You. And so is Greece. And so am I."

Athene comes to God.

"Signor?"
"Choo-Choo . . . how nice . . .
Congratulations on your victory."
"My what?"
"A clear, decisive, victory for your Greeks.
So that is that. Their champion she goes home,
The Sea can scrub that palisade, and peace can go the rounds."

King Agamemnon has stepped out and given his brother his sword,
He looks at Hector. Who will speak?
The armies wait.

"Pa-pa," Athene said—picking a cotton from his sleeve—
"This is not fairyland. The Trojans swore an oath
To which you put your voice."
"I did not."
"Father, you did. All Heaven heard you. Ask the Sea."

37

"I definitely did not."
"Did-did-did-did—and no returns."

Hector, Chylabborak, across the sand
Towards the brothers Atreus.

"Dearest Pa-pa, the oath said one should die.
The Trojan was about to die. He did not die.
Nobody died. Therefore the oath is dead.
Killed by a Trojan. Therefore Troy goes down."

Aeneas follows Hector, bypassing two
Drivers conducting underbody maintenance.

"Father, you must act.
Side with the Trojans, Greece will say,
Were we fools to believe in His thunder?
Why serve a God who will not serve His own?"

Hector and Agamemnon. Slope sees slope.
Such heat!

And giving her a kiss, He said:
"Child, I am God,
Please do not bother me with practicalities."

King Agamemnon says:
"Outstanding Prince, we live in miracles.
Our Lord and God, Whose voice dethrones the hills,
Has seen the woman won. Therefore I say,
Let her first husband have her, and her gold.
If not, I shall fill Troy with fire
And give its sobbings to the wind."

Still heat.
The Gate, all eyes.

Hector:

"Enemy King, I take your claim. Your brother Menelaos
Shall lead his wife, and that wife's gold, away.
And while she says goodbye, and Wall and plain
Wait till she walks across the sand into her husband's arms,
Let us, who fought for her together,
Make shade, and sit, and eat together,
Then listen to our story and shed tears
Together, for our dead, and for ourselves,
Among our horses and our hosts before we part,
You in your ships to your belovéd land,
We to our open city, or Beyond,
This afternoon, the favourable, on which,
In answer to my prayer, our rest began."

Rain over Europe.
Queen Hera puts her hate-filled face around its fall
And says to God:

"I want Troy dead.
Its swimming pools and cellars filled with limbs,
Its race, rotten beneath the rubble, oozing pus,
Even at noon the Dardanelles lit up,
All that is left a bloodstain by the sea."
    "Hold on . . ."
    "Shut up, you whelk."
    "Silence you both."
    "No, no," (wagging a finger in His face)

39

"I shall not stop. You shall not make me stop.
Troy asks for peace? Troy shall have peace. The peace of the dead—
Or you will have no peace until it does."

The terraces.
Teethee, her granny-slave, calls Helen with her head.

"Athene?"

Sniff.

God sighs and says:

"Magnificas,
You know how fond I am of Troy.
Its humans have acknowledged Me, and prayed to Me,
And raised high smoke to Me for centuries.
If I agree to your destroying it
And them, you must allow Me to destroy
Three Greek cities whose mortals have
Been faithful to yourselves as Troy to Me,
And when I do, remembering Troy, you will not say a word."

Their heads go close.

Below,
Cattle are being chosen for the feast.

Athene: "We accept.
Person for person, wall for wall,
Mycenae, Corinth, Sparta, match Troy's worth,
And they have prayed to us, etcetera,
For just as long as Ilus and his offspring have to you.
Let us kill Troy—do what you like with them."

"I can be comfortable with that," God said.
"Have the Nine sing again."

"Dear Shepherd of the Clouds," His sister said,
"I hate these quarrels just as much as you.
Send 'Thene to the plain, and while she finds
A Trojan fame-seeker to get the war
Back on the boil, and everything to normal once again,
Please be the god who is god to me."

But He had something more to say.
He stands: the Lord and Master of the Widespread Sky:

"After today,
On pain of being thrown into the void
To drift, alive, alone,
From universe to universe for all eternity,
The plain is closed to Heaven, including you too."
Cloud coral in deep seas. People with cameras.
Those sunlit chords.
"So child," (now smiling at Athene) "do
As my wifely sister says." And she
Cast herself earthwards with a shriek of joy
That echoed back as: "I know just the man!"

Note Pandar's facts:
Sired by lord Kydap of the Hellespont,
Competitive, north Ilium's star archer,
He likes to chat, but has a problem keeping off himself.
And now, as Hector says: "Make shade . . ." we centre him,
Practising bowpulls, running on the spot,
Surrounded by the shields he led to Troy.
                    But O,

41

As Hector reached " . . . our rest began . . ." a gleam
(As when Bikini flashlit the Pacific)
Staggered the Ilian sky, and by its white
Each army saw the other's china face, and cried:
  "O please!"
(As California when tremors rise)
  "O please!"
As through it came a brighter, bluer light
Gliding, that then seemed like a pair of lips
Hovering, and then a kiss, a nursing kiss
On Pandar's wide-eyed mouth, who closed his lids
And sipped its breath, and so became
The dreaded god Athene's host.

P andar has never felt so confident. So *right*.
His bow-slave, Deedam, massages his neck.
  "De-de, I am a man.
Like day is light is how I am a man.
But am I man enough, I ask myself,
To put a shot through Menelaos' neck,
While he is out there waiting for his wife?"
  "He is our enemy. Our duty is to kill him, Sir."
  "And their cause with him, De-de. Think of that."
  "Paris would give us a south tower, Sir."
  "Appropriate for a winning shot."
  "An unforgettable shot."
  Horses are being watered. Fires lit.
Such heat!
  "However, De-de, one thing is against it."
  "Sir?"
  "With their cause gone, the Greeks will sail,
So I shall lose my chance to kill Achilles."
  "In that case, Sir—"

"No, De-de, Troy comes first."
He stands.
"I have decided. I shall finish him now.
Prepare the Oriental bow, and I will pray."

The sweetwood roof.

"Until I closed our doorbolt," Cumin said,
"Old Teethee nattered about Paris' charm, his smile, etc.
Then all at once her squeaky words became
Spacious and clear.
    I sensed we were in trouble. Tu was green. At the same time
I wanted to be kissed and licked all over.
This is how Aphrodite sounds when she commands our flesh,
I told myself. And I was right. So we were lost.
But for the second time that day my lady acted like a king.
    Putting her beautiful world-famous face
Down into Teethee's crumpled face, and said:
    'I know your voice, lewd Queen. By using me
You aim to stymie lake-eyed Hera's spite.'—
Talking poor Teethee backwards around the floor—
    'So by a crossroads or a lake, a cave,
Only this morning catwalked for the son
Of some Nyangan cattle king whose Yes! to you
Has accessed him to me. Tu, Cumin—pack.
Make sure my pubic jewellery is all on top.
Yours, too. God only knows whose threesome we shall be.'—
Teethee now edging sideways down the wall.—
    'And all because the winner wants me back.
Lord Menelaos wants me back.
Oh yes he does. Oh yes he bloody does.
So your Judge Paris kisses me goodbye.
    Well, that's soon fixed

43

As you and he have such a meaningful relationship
Take my place. Of *course* you will give up your immortality:
Paradise dumped for love! Become a she—
How do I look? Will high heels help? And if,
If you try hard, your best, he may—note *may*—
Promote your exdivinity *Wife*. The apogee
Of standard amenties. No. That is wrong. I take that back.
Before the end of your productive life you bear
A *boy?*
Unfortunately not . . .
Why did you make me leave my land?
Look at me. All of you. My head is full of pain.
Ih!—there it goes. Pepper my breasts.
Why should I go to Paris. I am lost.'
Those were her words. And as the last of them
Fell from her downcast face, Teethee reached up
And with her fingers closed those vivid lips."

Then in that handsome room, in Troy, it was
Just as it is for us when Solti's stick comes down
And a wall of singers hits their opening note,
And the hair on the back of your neck stands up.
As she pulled Helen down, her form rose up
But not as Teethee's form, nor as Miss Must
Wringing her hair out, wet. But as she is:
A god. As Aphrodité, Queen of Love, her breasts
Alert and laden with desire in their own light,
Gloss of a newly-opened chestnut burr, her hair,
Her feet in sparkling clogs, her voice:
"Do stop this nonsense, Helen, dear.
You are not lost. You never shall be lost.
You are my representative on Earth.
You look around you—and you wait.
Try not to play the thankless bitch:

'Such a mistake to leave my land, my kiddywink . . .'
What stuff. Millions would give that lot
For half the looks that I have given you.
    You there: yes, you with the Egyptian eyes,
Prepare her bath. And you, Miss Quivering, strip her."
    They do as they are told.
    "Turn round."
Impartial as a sunbeam, her regard.
    "Your sweat, your wrinkle cream—quite useful. Eh?
Go through." And as they did:
    "You wear a crown of hearts. Your duty is
To stir and charm the wonder of the world.
To raise the cry: *Beauty is so unfair!*"
Leaves. Tiles. The sky. "And so it is.
Free. And unfair. And strong. A godlike thing."
The water's net across the water's floor.
    "Be proud. You have brought harm. Tremendous boys
Of every age have slaughtered one another
Just for you!" Tu works the loofah down her spine.
"And as God knows no entertainment quite
So satisfying as war, your name has crossed His lips . . ."
Now in a chair with one clog dangling.
"Think of it, Elly—crossed His lips. And one fine day
The richest city in the world will burn for you,
Lie on its side and cry into the sand for you—
But, Sweetie, do not be too quick to leave;
After that business with the palisade
The Sea will see no Greek worth mentioning gets home.

    "Dry her."
    We did.
    "Oil her."
    We did.
    "Dust her with gold.

45

Come here."
Tall, dignified, alone,
Wearing a long, translucent, high-necked dress.
Gold beads the size of ant-heads separate her girdle's pearls.
   "Bear this in mind:
Without my love, somewhere between the Greek and Trojan lines,
A cloud of stones would turn your face to froth.
So, when they lift the curtains, and he looks—you hesitate.
And then you say: Take me, and I shall please you."
   Pause.
"What do you say?"
"Take me, and I shall please you."
"Good. Now in you go."

Lord Pandar prays:

"Dear Lord of Archers and Dear Lady Lord,
Bare-breasted Artemis of Shots and Snares,
My blessings to You both
For blessing me with perfect sight
And for the opportunity to shoot
The Greek who caused this war
A man scarce worthy to be killed
By me, your gifted worshipper."

While his grey bow-slave slips the bowstring's eye
Over the bow's iron ear, then plucks its string,
And hearing—as his owner stands—the proper note,
Hands him the bow, and bows. Then stands well back
Watching his blameless fame-seeker assume
The best position for a vital shot.

The shields divide. Lord Pandar's shoulder blades
Meet in the middle of his back; the arrow's nock
Is steady by his nostril and its head
Rests on the bosom of the bow.
Someone has passed a cup to Menelaos,
And, as his chin goes up, child Pandar sights his throat,
Then frees the nock: and gently as the snow
Falls from an ilex leaf onto the snow
Athene left him, and the head moved out.

But the god did not forget you, Menelaos!
Even as she left, Athene tipped the shot
Down, past your brother,
—THOCK—
Into your pubic mound.

Wait for the pain, wait for the pain, and here it comes,
Wham! Wham!
" . . . aha . . ."

Shield shade. Field surgery.
Odysseus, Ajax, Thoal, tears in their eyes,
Then Makon, Panachea's surgeon, saying: "Shears."
" . . . aha . . ." (but soft) and,
Opening the loincloth (fishline rolled in silver),
There it is: in past its barbs,
A wooden needle resting in red wool, that Makon clips
" . . . aha . . ."
Then: "This" (the vinegar) "may sting." And as it did,
Paramount Agamemnon, King of kings,
Sighed as he knelt beside you on the sand,
And all his lords sighed, too, and all his underlords
Sighed, and though as yet they knew not why, the Greeks
All sighed as Makon cut, and Agamemnon said:
"I love you, Menelaos. Do not die. Please do not die."

47

(And cut) "for you are all I have.
And if you die the Greeks will sail" (and cut)
"Leaving my honour and your wife behind."
  Makon has nodded, and, as Jica kneels,
He and boy Aesculapius pull ". . . aha . . ."
The quadrilateral tabs of flesh his cuts have made
Back from the head for Jica's finger-strength to hold
Back and apart while Aesculapius swabs
And Makon looks, and Agamemnon says:
  "Oh, Menelaos. I have done so much
For your and Helen's sake, do not desert me now.
  You know what everyone will say. *He was a fool,*
When have the Trojans ever kept their word?
He should have done what they did—only first . . ."
Makon sits back . . . "And as the Fleet pulls out
The Trojans will parade her, and her gold,
Along the beach," the arrow-head has thrust
Into the cartilage coupling the pubic arch,
"But nobody will blame Odysseus
Although he organized the fight." And looking up
His brother said: "It may not be that bad . . ."
"It will be worse. I shall be treated like a strapless she.
Ignored. Pushed to one side." His head is in his hands.
  Now for the pain: as Jica parts the arch,
Makon will use his teeth his neck to draw
The head out of the gristle by its stump.
His face goes down. He breathes. He bites. He signs:
And smoothly as a fighter-plane peels off
". . . aha . . . aha . . ." (my God, that man takes pain,
As well as women do) lord Jica has the bones apart
And sweetly as he drew his mother's milk
Makon has drawn the barbed thing out
And dropped it into Aesculapius' hand,
Who looks (as he unlids the anaesthetic paste), says: "Clean."
Oh, stupid Pandar . . .

48

King Agamemnon stands.

His body shines. His face is terrible. His voice is like a cliff.
Taking a spear, and stepping, as his lords divide,
Out inbetween the slopes, he calls into the sky:

"Dear Lord, I know that you will not forget
The wine we poured, the lambs whose blood we shed,
And in Your own good time You will reduce
Truce calling Troy, truce spoiling Troy,
Oathmaking Troy, oathbreaking Troy,
Cowardly Troy, treacherous Troy to dust, to dust."

And now he takes a step, his lords behind,
Towards Hector, and he says:

"Bad Prince, God may take time. My time is now.
To shed your blood. To shed your dark red blood.
Your gleaming blood. And as you die,
The last thing that you see will be my jeering face,
The last voice that you hear, my voice,
Confiding how my heroes served your wife
And kicked your toddler off the Wall."

The terraces are empty.

The speaker turns
Back to his long bronze slope of men, and roars:

"There they are!"

"There they are!"

"The traitor race!"

49

"Let them die now!"

Raise your binoculars.
The dukes of Troy—Hector among them.
Hector's face. Faces near Hector's face.
Faces near Hector's face say *Now*. Who says:
"When God says strike, we strike—"
    Swing to the Greeks.
See them helping each other on with their bronze,
    Aeneas: "Now."
Fastening each other's straps.
    Sarpedon: "Now."
"—but I will recognize that moment when it comes."
Yet *Now* has caught his slope. And now,
Quibuph, holding his vulture-plumed helmet,
Catches his eye. Then with his silver yard
Poised by his lips, T'lesspiax, his trumpeter,
Catches his eye. And then it is his next,
Chylabborak, adding his *Now* to theirs.
    But we are not in fairyland.
We know that it was not till God turned to His son,
The Lord of Light and Mice, and said:
    "Let Thetis have her way,"
That Hector, whose clear voice
Rose like an arrow through the trembling air,
Cried:
    "Hearts, full hearts, courageous hearts,
Our lives belong to God and Ilium!" and waved them on—
Their flutes screeching across the thunder of their feet,
Their chariots deep in plumes—across the middle ground.
    But heroes are not frightened by appearances,
And as that bull-sea-roar of eight-foot shields came travelling on

The Greeks shook hands and said goodbye to one another,
Briefly, because the Trojan Wall-wide roar
  "Now!"
  "Now!"
Meant you could hardly hear a word you said.

  And when the armies met, they paused,
And then they swayed, and then they moved
Much like a forest making its way through a forest.
  And after ten years the war has scarcely begun,
And the god merely breathes for the Greeks to be thrown
(As shingle is onto a road by the sea)
Back down the dip, swell, dip of the plain.
  And now it has passed us the sound of their war
Resembles the sound of Niagara
Heard from afar in the still of the night.

Notes

My subtitle should continue: "plus material from Books Two, Five, Seven and Eleven of that poem"; as well, *The Husbands* includes a number of new scenes—Odysseus' subversion of Hector's challenge (pp. 11–13) and Athene's persuasion of God (pp. 37–38), for example. If, as a reader, you find some of the persons and the events mentioned in *The Husbands* obscure it is, I trust, because they have been established in its companion volumes, *Kings* and *War Music*.

page

9 "With blank, unyielding imperturbability" David Gascoygne, "The Bomb-site Anchorite," l. 20; in *An Enitharmon Anthology*, ed. Stephen Stuart-Smith, 1990.

10 "who was no prisoner" See Chaucer, *Troilus and Criseyde*, Bk. 4, st. 26.

13 "Murat" Joachim Murat, King Joachim I of Naples, Napoleon's principal cavalry commander.

14 "your voice is like an axe" See Bertrand Barère (Bertrand Barère de Vieuzac), *Memoirs* (translated by de V. Payen-Payne), vol. 4, p. 336, where he says of Saint-Just's (Louis-Antoine de Richebourg de Saint-Just) reports to the National Convention "They spoke like an axe," given as "He spoke like an axe" by Ian Hamilton Finlay and Richard Healy on their *card*, 1984.

15 "Hail and farewell" = "ave atque vale" See Catullus, *Poem 101*, an elegy to his dead brother, translated by Sir William Maris.

17 "cool their hooves" See Chapman, *Iliad*, Bk. 3, ll. 339–40.

18 "coclackia" A traditional Greek pebble mosaic laid as a floor surface, especially on terraces or in courtyards, and constructed by setting similarly sized pebbles in mortar; also applied to any exterior floor surface so constructed.

26 "Where the passing of the days is the only journey" = "Avec le file des jours pour unique voyage" Jacques Brel, "Le Plat Pays," *Jacques Brel*, Barclay LP 80173, Paris, 1962, translated by Rosemary Hill.

27 "Maginot Line" The system of fixed defences built by the French in the 1930s to protect their eastern frontier; named after André Maginot, a French politician.

42 "Each army saw" See Shakespeare, *Henry* V, Act 4, Prologue l.9.

42 "As through it came . . ." to " . . . a nursing kiss" See Tennyson, *Pelleas and Etarre*, ll. 36–38.

49 "long bronze slope" See Tennyson, "The Charge of the Heavy Brigade," l.17.

Guide to Pronunciation

Achilles	A·**kill**·eez
Aegean	A·**gee**·an
Aeneas	An·**ee**·us
Aesculapius	Ess·skull·**a**·pius
Agamemnon	Ag·a·**mem**·non
Akafact	**Aka**·fact
Andromache	An·**drom**·a·kee
Antilochos	An·**til**·o·kos
Aphrodite	Aph·ro·**dite**
and	
Aphrodité	Aph·ro·**di**·tee
Athene	Ah·**thi**·nee
Atreus	**Ay**·tre·us
Chylabborak	Chi·**lab**·bor·ak
coclackia	co·**clack**·ee·ah
Dardanelles	Dar·dan·**ells**
Dardanian	Dar·**day**·ni·an
Deedam	**Dee**·dam
Diomed	**Di**·oh·med
Dnepr	**Nee**·per
Hera	**He**·rah
Ilium	**Ill**·ee·um
Iwo Jima	Ee·woe **Jee**·mah
Jica	**Ji**·ka
Kykeon	Ky·**kee**·on
Laomedon	Lay·oh·**me**·don
Leto	**Lee**·tow
Makon	**Ma**·kon
Menelaos	Men·na·**lay**·us

Murat	**Moo**·rah
Mycenae	My·**sea**·nay
Nain	**Na**ne
Neomab	**Nee**·oh·mab
Odysseus	O·**diss**·ee·us
paean	pye·**an**
Pagif	**Pah**·gif
Panachean	Pan·ak·**ee**·an
Poseidon	Po·**sigh**·don
Priam	**Pry**·am
Quibuph	**Ki**·buff
Rhesos	**Ree**·soss
Sarpedon	Sar·**pee**·don
Schlacht	Schl·lacht
(like **tired**—1½ syllables)	
Skean	**Ski**·an
Talthibios	Tal·**thigh**·be·os
Tecton	**Tec**·ton
Teethee	**Tee**·thee
Thetis	**Theet**·is
Thoal	**Tho**·al
Tiryns	**Ti**·ryns
T'lesspiax	Tee·**less**·pee·ax